A

HISTORY

OF THE

BILLS OF CREDIT

OR

Paper Money issued by New York,

From 1709 to 1789:

WITH A

DESCRIPTION OF THE BILLS, AND CATALOGUE
OF THE VARIOUS ISSUES.

By JOHN H. HICKCOX.

AUTHOR OF AMERICAN COINAGE.

ALBANY, N. Y.:
J. H. HICKCOX & CO.
1866.

Edition 250 copies,
50 copies large paper in quarto.

J. Munsell, Printer.

INSCRIBED

TO

The Memory

OF

DR. T. ROMEYN BECK.

CONTENTS.

Early New York Paper Currency.

I.

The Early Currency of America.

The representative of currency used in America during the earlier period of colonization consisted of peltry and wampum.[1] The former was offered in almost unlimited quantities; the latter, called also *zewan* by the Dutch, held an arbitrary value for many years.[2] Both were repeatedly recognised as currency.[3] The necessity for coin only partially

[1] Said to be derived from *wampi*, signifying in Massachusetts Indian language—*white*. It was strung, and sometimes formed into belts.—*Encyc. Amer.*

[2] Its manufacture by the natives was necessarily rude. They commonly used the oyster and clam shell. The beads were bored with sharp stones, and strung upon sinews. The dark bead, less than an inch in length and bored longitudinally, was of the greatest value and more highly esteemed than European gold and silver. The Dutch somewhat improved it and made use of white and blue beads, which were manufactured from the sea conch and muscle. A string one fathom long was valued at four guilders, or one dollar sixty-six and one half cents of our currency—Munsell's *Annals.*

[3] *N. Y. Col. Docs.*, I, 87, 303; II, 594, 697, 703. *Albany City Records*, Sept. 23, 1686, etc.

existed, and its circulation in New Netherland, at least during the administration of the West India Company, was limited. Indeed a small amount was sufficient, as the general dealings of the community were by trade or barter. Beaver was for a long time the standard. Wampum never had a fixed value,[1] but varied from four to eight black beads for a stiver. The repeated complaints on the subject of its fluctuation seem to have been unheeded by the Directors of the Company, who would have the colonists consider it as good as bullion, yet would receive only beaver skins in payment of duties and taxes,[2] while supplies could be obtained only for beaver or silver.

That there was however at an early date a supposed scarcity of coin, appears from the fact that in 1642 the Council petitioned the Company to raise the value of money in order to prevent its exportation to foreign countries;[3] and at a later period Governor Stuyvesant endeavored to introduce a specie currency, and as one expedient proposed in imitation of New England, to establish a mint at New Amsterdam.[4] In 1673 there was little or no certain coin. Wampum passed for current payment, and it continued to constitute the currency of the com-

[1] *Col. Docs.*, III, 303.

[2] O'Callaghan's *New Netherland.*

[3] *Col. Docs.*, I, 203.

[4] *Manuscript Records*, Secretary's Office, IV, 387, 388.

mon or laboring people long after the colony ceased to belong to the Dutch.[1]

In most of the other provinces a barter trade was carried on similar to that of New Netherland. Wampum was introduced into New England by Isaac De Razier in 1627, and passed at the rate of 5*s.* per fathom. The General Court ordered in 1643, "that wampumpeag should pass current in the payment of debts to the amount of forty shillings." Besides this, English and Dutch coin, Indian corn, wheat, rye, barley, peas, live stock, beaver, bullets and gunpowder, constituted its currency during the early days of that colony.[2]

Virginia in 1618 made the following enactment—"All goods shall be sold at an advance of twenty-five per cent, and tobacco taken in payment at three shillings per pound, at not more or less, on the penalty of three years servitude to the colony."[3]—Other colonies at this date had simiar regulations;

[1] In 1683, the schoolmaster in Flatbush was paid his salary in wheat, "wampum value," and ten years later, the ferriage for each single person from New York to Brooklyn was eight stivers in wampum, or a silver two pence.—*O'Callaghan.*

[2] In Massachusetts (1631), the following enactment was made: "It is ordered that corne shall passe for payment of all debts at the usual rate it is solde for, except money or beaver be expressly named." Again in 1635—"It is ordered, that hereafter farthings shall not passe for currant pay. It is likewise ordered, that muskett bulletts of a full boare shall passe currently for a farthing a peece, provided that noe man be compelled to take above 12*d.* att a tyme of them."—*Mass. Records.*

[3] Holmes's *Amer. Annals.*

and as late as 1790 inspector's receipts for tobacco which had been lodged in the ware house, to await exportation, passed current as cash.

In Pennsylvania, about the year 1700, a proposition was brought before the General Assembly to make domestic products a legal tender, at their current rates, although according to one account[1] specie was more plentiful in that province than in England. As late as 1732 in Maryland, an act was passed making tobacco a legal tender at one penny per pound, and Indian corn at twenty cents per bushel.

[1] Thomas's *Account of Pennsylvania*, 1698.

II.

THE INTRODUCTION OF PAPER MONEY INTO AMERICA.

The introduction of paper money into America, as a medium of exchange, was made in Massachusetts. Prior to the year 1652 bills passed current in the payment of debts.[1] In this year, the subject was discussed in the General Court with the view of increasing the facilities of trade. No enactment followed, but we find an approximation to it in 1675 in the following record: "For the prevention of the charge and trouble of transportation of the rates to be leveyed, to the treasurer of the county, as also matter of convenience therein appearing, it is ordered that bills for wages, horses, provisions, &c., being regularly passed to the sayd treasurer, the Treasurer upon the desire of persons concerned shall repass bills to the constables of such townes, where sums are due upon the aforesaid accounts."[2]

In 1686, during the presidential government of New England, permission was granted to John Blackwell of Boston, and others, residents of Eng-

[1] Felt's *Account of Massachusetts Currency.*

[2] *Massachusetts Records.*

land as well as of this country, to commence the issuing of bank-bills "on the security of real and personal estate and imperishable merchandize." How far and how long the operations of this corporation were carried on, is not precisely known.

It was in 1690 that the first issue of paper money was made by an American colony. New England and New York undertook to drive the French from Canada. The expedition failing, the soldiers returned sooner than was expected, and were clamorous for their pay, and being unwilling to await the time necessary to raise a revenue by a direct tax, the authorities of Massachusetts resolved in the emergency to issue a paper currency, and thereupon directed a committee to prepare immediately bills to the amount of £7,000.[1] Many precautions were made in order to preserve their value, but depreciation speedily followed their issue. The government received them at par in payment of taxes, and added five per cent to the principal, so that they soon became objects of speculation.

The next colony which issued paper money was Carolina, the necessity for which grew out of an expedition against St. Augustine in 1702. Bills of credit to the amount of £6,000 were issued, to be cancelled in three years, by a duty laid upon liquors, skins and furs. In 1705 or 1706 a paper money act

[1] According to Hutchinson these bills were issued in notes from 2*s*. to £10. Mr. Felt says from 5*s*. to £5.

was passed in the island of Barbadoes. These three instances are believed to be the only enactments creating bills of credit in the British American colonies prior to the acts passed in Connecticut at the session begun in May, 1709, and in New York, June 8th, of the same year.

III.

THE PAPER MONEY OF NEW YORK.

New Netherland was surrendered to the English in 1664, the Duke of York having obtained a grant of the province from King Charles II. The Dutch reconquered the country, but it was eventually restored to the English in 1674, when the Duke obtained a new grant of the colony of New York. The government was composed of the governor and council appointed by the king, and subsequently of the assembly chosen by the people. In it was vested the authority to make laws, subject to the approval of the proprietary. The General Assembly convened for the first time in 1682.

Difficulties in regard to the currency of the province existed at an early date. The coins of Holland, France, Germany, Spain, England and a remnant of the Massachusetts coinage carried with them each the distinct valuations made in their respective countries. As has already been stated, wampum circulated for a long time as the colonial currency, but it gradually disappeared as trade and prosperity increased, when the revenue for the support of government was derived from crown rents, forfeitures, taxation,[1] duties, the emission of paper money and lotteries.

After the first reduction of New Amsterdam, the necessary means to defend it against the Dutch and Indians exhausted the money and credit of the colony.[2] Trade became much reduced, and supplies from England were protracted and small. Even the private resources of the governor were exhausted. He complained that "he was utterly ruined in his small estate and credit." During the administration of Gov. Andros frequent efforts were made to increase the supply of money, which was represented as insufficient for an ordinary commerce. The importation of British brass farthings, restamping Spanish pieces-of-eight,[3] the special coinage of a few thousand pounds for circulation in the province, were plans severally suggested, neither of which received material encouragement. Gov. Dongan, and subsequently the Earl of Bellomont,[4] recommended the establishment of a mint, which suggestion the duke's commissioners signified their will-

[1] The first internal tax in New York (New Netherland) was levied in 1644, and was for the purpose of meeting the expense incurred by the Indian wars.

[2] In raising 300 men for the protection of the frontier, it was found necessary to require each county to raise, pay and maintain their own men, according to the proportion then agreed upon.

[3] 1675.

[4] Aug. 27, 1684 and 1700.

ingness to consider, but no further notice appears to have been taken of it.

The low state of the currency it was thought, arose from the fact that most of the foreign trade came through Boston and other places of the East, which tended to draw in that direction the money as well as produce. In view of such facts the merchants of New York petitioned the general assembly for enactments which it was imagined would increase the supply of currency. It was, in fact, injudicious legislation which had already removed the currency from the province; it was now proposed that no wheat should be exported from the province save only for the Madeira Islands; that the ten per cent. formerly laid upon all European goods that did not come directly from England hither, over and above the two per cent. already imposed, should again be required.

The instructions from the government were stringent and reiterated that no alteration should be made in the value of current coin. It was nevertheless subject to constant change, for we find that in 1695, the difference between New York and sterling money was about one fifth, and in 1700 about one quarter. Difficulties were increased too by the diverse values held in the several colonies. Pieces of eight of the value of 6*s.* passing in New York for 6*s.* 9*d.*, in New Jersey for 7*s.* 8*d.*, in Maryland for 4*s.* 6*d.*, and in Virginia and Carolina for 5*s.* To relieve these embarrassments the queen in 1705, issued a proclamation settling and ascertaining the current rates of coin in the plantations.

Against this the merchants of New York remonstrated on the ground of the frauds committed under it, inasmuch as in some of the provinces the proclamation was duly published, but no notice taken of it. Lord Cornbury was induced to take the responsibility of suspending it. The assembly afterwards assumed the right to settle the value of coin in a manner to meet the view of the colonists, for which proceeding it was censured by the government.

A few years later (1708) the legislature passed an act regulating and preventing the corruption of the current coin, which, although favorably commended by Lord Cornbury, was reported against by the lords of trade on the ground that coin was raised to a higher rate than was allowed by the act of parliament and the proclamation. It was subsequently vetoed, and the veto published in New York and New Jersey. The legislature, however, disregarded the veto, and resolved to pass no bill for money for the support of government unless at the rates contained in the vetoed bill. Governor Hunter dissolved the house several times, but to no purpose; both he and all the government officers remained without support for a number of years. He was finally under the necessity of conceding, and the assembly appointed a treasurer to receive and pay all money granted to the king and the province, in place of the king's receiver general. A few years later, parliament having passed an act regulating, on a uniform scale, the rates of foreign coin in the plantations, the general assembly remonstrated on the ground that if money passed at the same rates here as at the West Indies, it would not be worth the merchant's while to bring the money, but rather the produce of those islands in return for our produce; and as our principal commerce was to those parts, there would not be brought back money enough to support either the government or commerce. It was claimed that the effect of both the proclamation and the act of parliament would be to establish in the colonies a depreciated currency, and drive all the gold and silver coin to England, and it was urged, therefore, that assent should be given to an act which the assembly had recently passed, regulating the currency of the colony. This act provided that Spanish pieces should not pass at less than eight shillings per oz., troy—whereas the proportion in the act of parliament was 6*s.* 10*d.* In the absence of the royal assent, the governor, as requested, ordered the execution of the latter (New York) act.[1]

As has already been stated, New England and New York undertook, at the instance of the British government, to drive the French from Canada, circular letters having been addressed by the officer of

[1] It was subsequently reported against by the board of trade, and vetoed by the queen.

the crown to the governors of the American colonies, directing them to assist in carrying on the expedition. A proposition was immediately passed upon in the house of assembly of New York[1] to raise 487 men as her quota for this purpose. It was enacted that a tax of £6,000 should be levied, but as funds were needed immediately, another act followed[2] enforcing the currency of bills of credit to the amount of £5,000. This was the first paper currency act passed in New York.

Although New England, New Jersey, and Pennsylvania joined New York in this operation against Canada, the latter contributed more than any of the other colonies. In the New Jersey and Pennsylvania legislatures the Quakers voted against the appropriations, and in the former colony defeated them, but subsequently the bill was reconsidered and passed. The expense incurred by New York was above £20,000.[3] Other enactments creating bills of credit for the same object, followed the one already mentioned. In November, 1709,[4] two were passed, one for the currency of bills to the amount of £4,000, another for ten thousand ounces of plate, or fourteen thousand five hundred and forty-five

[1] May 25, 1709.

[2] June 8, 1709.

[3] Smith's History.

[4] November 1st and 12th, 1709.

Lyon dollars[1] (equal to £4,000). These bills were for a short time received by the treasurer at their value with an advance of 2½ per cent. from the date of the bill to the day the treasurer received them. The regulation, as had been the case in Massachusetts, induced many to hold them on account of the accumulating interest; but at the next session an act was passed forbidding the treasurer or any other person paying or receiving any interest on their account. The bills then issued, as well as those emitted subsequently, were cancelled as they were paid in. To counterfeit them was felony without benefit of clergy.

Although the expedition against Canada was unsuccessful, a few operations in Nova Scotia and Newfoundland which had resulted favorably, stimulated a renewed attack against the former. Assistance arrived from England and Flanders. The general assembly convened, and the subject was brought before it. Some dissatisfaction arose as to the large proportion required of New York, but in a few days[2] an act was passed to raise a force of 600 men in connection with 360 from Connecticut, 360 from the Jerseys, and 240 from Pennsylvania. A new issue of bills of credit was ordered to the amount of 25,000 ounces of plate, or £10,000, to

[1] The value of Lyon dollars in 1711 was 13 pwt. 18 gr.; in 1720, 15 pwt.

[2] July 26, 1711.

defray the expense. They were to be current not longer than eight years. Every collector of taxes was required to indorse on the bill the date of payment, after which time the bill so endorsed was no longer current.

Owing to bad management, and the wreck of a number of vessels, failure ensued, the troops returning home without even an encounter.

The state of affairs in New York at this time, was by no means harmonious. Discouraged by recent disasters, the ill feeling between the governor, council, and assembly, manifested itself on several occasions. The province was largely indebted to individuals for money and effects, advanced for the service of the army. Provision had been made by former governors for the payment of a great part of these claims, out of the funds which had been from time to time raised for the support of government. Warrants had been signed and issued, but the sums having been misapplied, the debts remained upon the colony: the government credit was low, and the inhabitants quite discouraged.

In order to relieve difficulties, which were daily becoming more complicated, an act was passed in 1712, under which commissioners were appointed to examine and state the several debts claimed to be due from the government. In order to discharge the debts thus ascertained, another act was passed in 1713, laying an excise on all strong liquors retailed in the colony. It was to continue in force from 1714 to 1734, and the money arising thereby, appropriated to discharge the public debts, as subsequently directed. Nearly the whole session of 1714, was consumed in discussing the subject. Governor Hunter informed the assembly, that he would pass no law until provision was made for the relief and support of government. The assembly finally yielded, and passed an act[1] "for paying and discharging the several debts and sums of money claimed as debts of this colony to the several persons therein named, and to make and enforce the currency of bills of credit, to the value of £27,680 for that purpose; also to make void all claims and demands made, or pretended to be due from this colony, before the first of June, 1714, and to prevent this colony from being in debt for the future." The several sums appropriated, were to be paid in bills of credit, the claimants to accept them in full satisfaction of what was respectively due to, or claimed by them. The bills were to be accepted in all payments of debts, as gold or silver, thereby constituting them a legal tender. The loss of such debt, and a perpetual bar from its recovery, was the penalty for refusing such payment. Any person who should offer to sell any kind of property, and refuse to sell the same unless

[1] Sept. 4, 1714, known as the "1st Long Bill."

payment be made in coin, was fined from 40*s*. to £50, and costs, according to the value of the article offered. The bills were not issued before this act, as well as the act laying the excise, were confirmed by her majesty, which was accomplished in June, 1717.

The statute excluded all who were not expressly named therein, from recovering any claim for debts due by the colony, before the 1st of June, 1714, and objections were justly urged against its approval. An explanatory act was therefore passed in 1715, which provided that nothing in the said act, which had excluded *all future demands* whatsoever, should be construed to hinder, bar, or exclude any person having any just claim or demand, from pursuing and obtaining relief.

For the purpose of repairing the fortifications, and for other necessities of government, an act was passed on the 5th of July, 1715, levying duties on certain articles, authorizing the emission of bills of credit to the value of 15,000 ounces of plate, equal to about £6,000, to be current for five years,[1] and to be canceled by the treasurer retaining annually, in the first instance 3,000 oz. of plate from the revenue arising from taxes. It was enforced without the royal approval. The lords of trade refused to submit it to the king, because it seemed repugnant

[1] Afterwards extended to nine years.

to the act of parliament, settling the rates of foreign coin in the plantations. By the latter act, pieces of eight were not to pass for more than 6*s*., whereas by the New York enactment an ounce of plate was valued at 8*s*. Should the royal approval, said they, be given, the other governments on the continent would immediately do the same thing, and the intent of the act of parliament would be wholly evaded. To which objection the governor replied that the bill was framed after the same manner as to the value of coin, with that for the payment of the public debts, which his majesty, by means of their lordships' recommendation, had approved: that the matter could in no way affect the neighboring colonies, because they had never yet complied with the proclamation. The bills having become widely dispersed before the objections of the lords of trade were communicated, and on account of the bad results which would ensue both to the credit of the colony and to commerce, from a disallowance, it was permitted to lie by, until the expiration of the time fixed for the currency of the bills issued under its authority.

Under the provisions of the law passed in 1715, commissioners had been appointed to adjust and state the several debts still due by the colony. They now laid their account before the assembly. It having been resolved to discharge the whole and to raise such sums as would be necessary for this and other purposes, a law was passed[1] raising and putting into the hands of the treasurer several quantities of plate, and making bills of credit to the value of 41,517 oz., equal to £16,607; and for sinking them a duty of 1¼ oz. of plate was laid on every ton of wine, and 2½ grs. on every gallon of rum, brandy, and other distilled liquors imported for 17 years.

A vigorous remonstrance was made against the passage of this act, by merchant-traders and others, for the most part non-residents of the province, partly from opposition to the excise, and partly from the more general encouragement to trade to the prejudice of the few who had so long monopolized it. An agent was employed to procure, if possible, its disallowance. Gov. Hunter urged his personal protest against their objections to the bill, which he characterized as the most unexceptionable that was ever passed. The lords of trade referred the remonstrance to the lords justices, who reviewing the action of the legislature, and the necessities existing for the currency, were unanimously of the opinion that the act should be confirmed; at the same time recommending that the governor be enjoined not to give his assent to any other bill of this nature, and to transmit semi-annually, accounts of the produce of the funds appropriated for sinking the bills of

[1] Dec. 23, 1717. Known as the "2d Long Bill."

credit, and the amount of the bills accordingly sunk.

Under the operations of this law, the currency being based on so solid a fund as that of the excise, trade and navigation were favorably affected. The bills of New York were twenty-five to thirty per cent better in New England than their own, being equal to silver, and in some of the neighboring provinces, fifty per cent better.

The administration of Governor Burnet began on the 17th of September, 1720. A supply for five years was granted him, and a law passed[1] directing to be printed forthwith, bills of credit to the value of 5,000 oz. of plate (equal to £2,000). It subsequently appearing that the revenue was insufficient for the large amount of these, and other bills required annually to be canceled, owing partly to a deficiency in the duties, their currency was continued by later enactments, to Sept. 1, 1733, and in the meantime increased taxes were levied.

In 1723 and 1724,[2] acts were passed "for raising and levying 5,350 oz. of plate (about £2,140), and for striking bills of credit to that value;" also, "for raising and levying the sum of £6,630," mainly for the payment of government charges, the greater part to supply the deficiency in the revenue, which

[1] Nov. 19, 1720.

[2] July 6, and July 24.

arose from the arrears of fees due to the auditor general; the balance, for promoting a trade with the Indians, which was encouraged by keeping up a constant supply of traders at the public expense.[1] The currency of these bills was restricted to three years.

The trade of the colony at this time was chiefly with Great Britain and the British plantations in the West Indies, although it extended to Madeira, Curaçoa, Surinam and the French Islands. That to the West Indies was wholly to the advantage of New York, while that to Madeira was to our loss, the province consuming more wine from thence than could be purchased with its commodities. The money imported from the West Indies was not sufficient however to preserve a specie currency, a large amount being necessary to balance the exchange with Great Britain. It seldom remained here long, so that the currency consisted wholly of paper bills and a few Lyon dollars.[2] The value of the former was equal in New York to coin in London, an ounce of Spanish pieces-of-eight being worth but sixpence more than a paper bill of eight shillings, and an ounce of Spanish silver in London being generally worth three or four pence sterling more than the coin.

Many of the bills in circulation, and particularly

[1] *Col. Docs.*, v. 701.

[2] *Col. Docs.*, v, 686.

those of the smaller denomination became in time so defaced and torn as to be illegible and almost worthless. On four separate occasions[1] therefore, new issues amounting to £19,000 were made and lodged in the state treasury to be exchanged for bills of this description. The preamble of the act of 1726 cites, that the service of signing these re-issues was to be *gratuitous*[2]. These bills are distinguished from the others by an oval blank at the top, in which the date of the original bill is written.

For the space of ten years (1724 to 1734) no new bills of credit were created excepting those last described. In the spring of 1734 the governor recommended several measures for putting the colony in a better state of defence. The position of affairs in Europe indicated a rupture between England and France. With a view to these contingencies he urged the erection of proper fortifications on the frontiers, and in the harbor of New York.

His suggestions met the approval of the legislature, and after a long preamble citing the various causes which had heretofore called for the issue of paper money, and assuring the public that the credit of the colony was still unimpaired, that the

[1] July 24, 1724, £3,000; Nov. 11, 1727, £3,000; Oct. 17, 1730, £3,000; Oct. 25, 1739, £10,000.

[2] An allowance of £8 was usually made for numbering and signing the bills.

campaign in Canada could not have been carried on without the help of a paper credit, and that it would be impracticable to fortify the colony unless the same expedient was made use of, it was enacted[1] that bills of credit to the value of £12,000 should be printed and lodged in the treasury.

This measure much gratified his excellency who hoped by the patronage it carried, to weaken the opposition which was then existing. The standing instruction from the king required however, as has been already stated, a clause in every bill, suspending its operations until his majesty's approval could be known. In order that none of the governor's aims should be thwarted, his friends in the council induced the house to appoint a committee to meet them and prepare an address requesting him on account of urgent necessity to pass the bill. It was immediately prepared, and on the next day presented and passed, but not without opposition.

The bills issued by this act, were to be current for twenty-two years, and to be canceled by a duty on tonnage or goods, and a tax on slaves.

Trade had for some time been on the decline. Merchants having the means, chose rather to make loans at eight per cent, which was considered an excessive rate, than to engage in commerce. Besides, imports were considerably taxed, being charged with almost the whole support of government.

[1] Nov. 28, 1734.

The merchants suggested a tax on lands, but the members from the country being in the majority, prevented the adoption of such a plan. There was a disposition to increase the currency by a new emission of paper money, but the great poverty of the province and its inability to bear further taxation was given as the excuse. The opposition was made in reality by the moneyed interest, for it was generally understood that it was postponed to create a *loan* at a lower rate of interest than money commanded.[1]

The spring session of 1737 found the province involved largely in debt which had arisen from an insufficiency of former revenues. Amounts were due the late governor, the chief justices and other officers, for salaries, to the amount of about £9,000. The lieut. governor, who was then acting, urged the immediate attention of the house to the matter, intimating that unless aid was provided, the people would have an opportunity of electing new representatives. After waiting about a month for their favorable action and no relief tendered, he summoned them to his council chamber, and in a short speech dissolved them.

The new assembly had a spring session of only a few days. At its reopening in the fall, the lieut.

[1]The present legal rate of interest (7 per cent) was established by law in 1738. It was proposed in the assembly, to make it 6 per cent, but the council altered it to 7.

governor again commended an honorable revenue for the support of the government. This session, which was a long one, resulted in the passage on its last day,[1] of an act emitting bills of credit to the amount of £48,350, which was a consequence unanswerable to the late election. Still, the assembly wishing to place itself as not countenancing prodigality, assured his excellency that he was not to expect that they either would raise sums unfit to be raised, or put what they should raise in the power of the governor to misapply if they could prevent it; nor would they make up any other deficiency than they should conceive fit and just to be paid, or continue what support or revenue they should raise for any longer time than *one year*. Much to the annoyance of the governor, they did not omit to act up to their determination, and the system thus inaugurated was continued by subsequent assemblies, although every argument was employed to induce a return to the former custom of granting supplies for five years.

This law was different from any of the preceding in several important particulars. As it contemplated an increase of the circulating medium, which had become quite reduced,[2] the currency of the neighboring colonies having become the chief medium of

[1] Dec. 16, 1737. The act was known as the "Loan Bill."

[2] Small change was so scarce that coppers were imported from England as a profitable speculation.—*Col. Docs.*, VI, 117.

trade, the sum of £40,000 was reserved as a *loan*, to be distributed among the several counties in the following proportions:

New York, ...	£10,000	Kings, ...	£2,400
Suffolk, ...	3,000	Richmond, ...	1,600
Dutchess, ...	2,000	Orange, ...	2,000
Albany, ...	5,000	Ulster, ...	4,000
Queens, ...	6,000	Westchester, ..	4,000

the interest of which was annually applied to the support of government. The office of "loan commissioner" was created, and the commissioners were required to loan the amounts thus apportioned on the security of mortgage on real estate, at an annual interest of five per cent, for the term of twelve years, in sums not to exceed £100, nor less than £25. They were also authorized to loan sums for one year, on the security of good plate at six shillings per ounce. At the expiration of the time allowed for the circulation of these bills, they were to be returned to the treasurer, and canceled. The sum of £8,350, appropriated for the payment of government debts, was to be sunk in part by certain taxes due from several counties, and the balance from interest accruing on the £40,000 loan.[1]

The currency of the bills emitted in 1714 and 1717, amounting to £44,287 was now soon about to expire.

[1] The bills of 1734 of the denomination of 10 and 5 shillings, and of 1737 of the denomination of 40 shillings, were counterfeited in Ireland.

About one half of the amount was still in circulation. Gov. Clark, well aware that the assembly would attempt to extend the term, as well as the excise act, for a sufficient number of years to allow of the extinction of the bills, endeavored to force the house to abrogate the system of yearly supplies for the support of government, as well as the special application of the funds. He perceived the necessity the assembly would be put to, and repeatedly assured the lords of trade that he would on no consideration yield until he had "brought them to their senses." He intimated to the legislature, therefore, that he would pass no bill allowing such an extension, unless a supply for at least five years was granted; whereupon the house resolved not to pass even the *annual* supply bill, without assurances that the paper money of the dates above mentioned, and the excise bills, should be continued for some years. Clauses were attached to the supply bill to this effect, and a committee appointed to inform the governor of their action. The next day he summoned the assembly, and reviewing their action, informed them that they had taken such "presumptuous, daring, and unprecedented steps," that he could not look upon them without astonishment, nor with honor suffer them to sit any longer.

Writs for a new election were issued returnable on the 27th of March 1739. Scarcely a week elapsed from the opening of the session before the bill which had occasioned the late rupture was introduced, considered soon after, and passed. Apprehending that it might not receive the governor's approval, the assembly passed a resolution to support the credit of the paper emissions of the colony, and especially those of 1714 and 1717, declaring at the same time, that they did not doubt but that future assemblies would do the same. The lieut. governor, highly indignant, at once prorogued this body also with the following speech:

"Gentlemen:—I come to put an end to this session, and to give you a short recess. I was in hopes, and I believe every reasonable man expected that at this juncture you would seriously have laid to heart the true interests of your country by showing your duty and loyalty to his majesty in supporting his government in an honorable manner."

The prorogation was for one week. The day following their reassembling, the bill entitled "An act further to continue the duty of excise and the currency of the bills of credit emitted thereon," was read a second time (having been introduced and read on the previous day) and committed to a committee with instructions to add clauses for the emission of new bills of credit to be exchanged for those which had become torn and defaced. It went rapidly through the two houses, and on the

25th of October, 1739,[1] received the lieut. governor's *assent*, with this brief message:—"I am come to give my assent to the bills that are ready for it, as the highest instance I can give of my care for the credit and welfare of the colony, and the confidence I have in your honor."

The reverse in the governor's determination was induced by several circumstances. He was convinced that the country was quite unanimous in approving the course of the assembly, and that a new election would only result, as it had already, in the return of men not otherwise minded than their predecessors. Again, there were appearances of a rupture between England, France and Spain, and he wished to avail himself of the assembly's present sitting, to place the province in a proper state of defence; and finally, because the assembly had become still more resolute in their intentions, from a recent example in the province of New Jersey, where the governor had given his consent to a revenue bill whereby the money was all *specially* applied.[2] To these reasons should be added, personal necessities, the usual supplies having been so long

[1] The bills emitted by this act have been already alluded to—see p. 22.

[2] In former acts no applications had been made of the funds, except for the salaries of treasurer and members of assembly:—the remainder being generally appropriated "for the support of his majesty's government."

withheld that the governor had even sold some of his estates to enable him to support the government.[1] He apologized to the lords of trade for his unexpected action, on the ground of the precedent set in New Jersey, but asked their favorable allowance of the bills on account of the feeling existing in the province, assuring them that he had thereby secured a greater state of quiet than had been known for forty years before.

On the representations of London, Liverpool and Bristol merchants, in June, 1739,[2] a series of resolutions were introduced in parliament, praying his majesty that an account might be prepared of the rate at which gold and silver coins were taken and paid in any of the British colonies in America; also of the amount of paper bills issued in any of said colonies since the year 1700, the provisions made for sinking them, and the amount canceled: to which resolutions, the commissioners of trade and plantations responded,[3] laying before parliament returns quite full, which had been received in answer to inquiries, from eleven of the colonies.

The proceedings excited the attention of most of the provinces, and their agents in London were instructed to petition the house of commons for a

[1] *Col. Docs.*, VI, 160.

[2] House of Common's Journals.

[3] March 28, 1740.

hearing in the matters referred to, and to use their best endeavors to procure the postponement of any unfavorable bill. The subject was temporarily disposed of by declaring that the instructions of his majesty, and the laws of parliament, regarding the rates of foreign coins in the plantations had not been observed. The instruction was renewed not to allow any bill to pass, whereby bills of credit might be issued in lieu of money, without a clause inserted declaring that the act should not take effect until approved by the king.

It has been already noticed that these instructions were not strictly enforced in the colony of New York, and the same was probably true in respect to other colonies ;accordingly in 1744 the complaint was renewed that large emissions of bills of credit had been made, notwithstanding the "instructions," and that more were intended. Whereupon leave was granted to bring in a bill to prevent the issuing of paper bills of credit in the British colonies and plantations in America, to be legal tenders in payments of money, which bill having had its first reading was indefinitely postponed.

No public measures were taken in the general assembly of New York to controvert these proceedings in parliament, but her interests were nevertheless well cared for. It had been rumored in the assembly before the conclusion of the fall session of 1745, that such a measure was before the house of commons. The credit of our bills was quite unimpaired and it was not conjectured that any objections could be urged against them in parliament. No copy of the bill under consideration had been seen here, and it was not until after the adjournment when one was borrowed from a neighboring colony, that the last clauses which were especially offensive, were fully comprehended. Indignation was at once aroused in every mind, for to use the words of the committee, "If all the parts of the legislature in every colony and plantation should be obliged and enjoyned (as by the said clauses are directed) to pay strict obedience to such orders and instructions as should from time to time be transmitted to them or any of them by his majesty or his successors, or by or under his or their authority, it would establish such an absolute power in the crown, in all the British plantations, as would be inconsistent with the liberties and privileges inherent in a Englishman whilst he is in a British dominion."

Without delay a meeting of several members of the council and merchants resident in New York was called, and it was determined not to allow such measures to go through parliament without at least a protest. Funds were advanced to employ a solicitor and counsel in London to oppose the bill before the committee of the house of commons. The general assembly at its next session fully recognized these proceedings, officially acknowledging the services of the agents, and refunded the amounts advanced for their services.

To defray the expense of carrying on the war against the French and Indians, in conjunction with the Eastern colonies, a law was passed in 1746 (May 3) to raise a supply of £13,000 by a tax on estates real and personal, and to emit bills of credit for the like sum. The amount was to be canceled in three years by an annual tax, in the proportion indicated in the following table:

New York,.......	£1,444	8s.	11d.
Albany,.........	622	3s.	9½d.
Kings,...........	254	18s.	0½d.
Queens,.........	487	9s.	5½d.
Suffolk..........	433	6s.	8d.
Richmond,......	131	6s.	3½d.
Westchester,...	240	14s.	8½d.
Ulster,...........	393	18s.	9½d.
Orange,..........	144	8s.	10½d.
Dutchess,........	180	11s.	11½d.

A new issue was soon after made, and for the same purpose. The colony's funds had been anticipated and exhausted, and a heavy tax remained unpaid. To use the language of the assembly, "it was constrained, but with the greatest regret," to make a further issue at this time.

A scheme for the conquest of Canada was again brought forward. Orders had been sent over by the British government directing the colonies to raise as many volunteers as the time would permit, to join the regular forces from England. The governor recommended that the most ample provision should be made and in the most speedy manner. The assembly perceiving that the movement was popular with the people, seconded most enthusiastically the demand for men and means. "Willing rather to exceed than to fall short in supplies on this important occasion" they promptly enacted,[1] that the sum of £40,000 should be raised by an annual tax of £5,000 on real and personal estate, and that to answer the immediate payment of the sums required, bills of credit to the full amount should be issued. This amount proving insufficient, the following year,[2] another act was passed, creating £28,000 to be paid by a yearly tax of £3,500.[3]

Circumstances growing out of the control and disbursement of these funds, occasioned controversies to which in point of bitterness, modern political warfare affords no parallel. The assembly assumed the right of judging of the necessities of the colony, and moreover took advantage of the demands and actual necessities of the government to secure for their own friends positions of power and influence. Governor

[1] July 15, 1746.

[2] Nov. 25, 1747.

[3] Bounties were raised for volunteers, and the exportation of provisions suspended. The neighboring Indians also were incited to aid in the enterprise.

Clinton, anxious to carry out the wishes of his government, was compelled to make concessions, and explanations of the manner in which funds and provisions previously granted had been applied. The bill was passed, but the distribution of the means for carrying on the expedition was intrusted to commissioners.

The governor, on the advice of the council, assented to the act notwithstanding the opposing "instructions," because the extraordinary occasion seemed to require it, and then dissolved the general assembly. In his letter to the lords of trade of this date, he recounts his grievances, and deprecates the growing power of the assembly, and suggests as a remedy the repeal of the acts issuing bills of credit and reissuing these bills under such conditions as his majesty should think proper.

This disagreement between the governor and general assembly continued for several years. The former attempted a restoration of the appropriation of supplies for the government for five years as in the times of Hunter, Burnet, &c., which was successfully resisted by the latter, as were efforts to reinvest the governor with certain privileges now claimed by the assembly. On a subsequent occasion the treasurer refused to furnish the governor with a statement of the accounts of the colony or of the bills of credit, in order to enable him to respond to a demand from the crown.

Between the years 1748 and 1752 there was peace between France and England. The long contests for possessions in America had resulted partially favorable to the latter. Vast amounts of money had been expended by the colonies for the honor of the crown. New York alone had contributed up to this time more than £81,000 without demanding or receiving any reimbursement,[1] as had been the case in some of the other colonies. The amount which she had issued since the commencement of the bills of credit system, although quite large, had not yet brought about the disastrous consequences which had befallen some of the neighboring provinces where proper precautions for canceling had not been taken. The emissions and rëemissions in Massachusetts alone from 1702 to 1740 amounted to £1,442,500, and at the latter date £230,000 were still outstanding. Its depreciation was alarming. In 1700 the colonial pound was worth $2.90 of Massachusetts money; in 1727, $1.48; in 1734, 91 cents; in 1738, 78 cents, was finally reduced to $\frac{1}{10}$ of a pound sterling.[2] In respect to the colonies in general, the following table exhibits the rate of exchange for £100 sterling at two different periods.

[1]Two small grants were subsequently made by the British parliament.

[2] *Essex Inst. Hist. Coll.* 1, 128.

	1740.		1748.
New England,	£525,	......	£1,100,
New York,	160,	......	190,
New Jersey,	160,	......	180, & 190,
Pennsylvania,	170,	......	180,
Maryland,	200,	......	200,
North Carolina,	1,400,	......	1,000,
South Carolina,	800,	......	750,
Virginia,	——	......	120, & 125.

The result of unsafe and extravagant issues in the eastern provinces was the passage of an act by parliament in 1751, regulating and restraining paper bills of credit in Rhode Island, Connecticut, Massachusetts and New Hampshire, and preventing the same from being a legal tender. The enactment forbade the use of such money except for yearly government expenses, and in case of invasion, and not at all as a legal tender for debts. Any governor who should sanction a law having a different signification should be deprived of his office, and ever after be ineligible to public employment.

The interim of peace between England and France afforded an opportunity for maturing new projects for conquest in America. France having no frontier coast, set about consummating a plan to possess the St. Lawrence and the Mississippi, and to establish a line of forts through the interior of the country. These operations were looked upon as

[2] Gough on Banking.

encroachments, and on the complaint of the Ohio company, whose province had been trespassed upon, Governor Dinwiddie, of Virginia, called for desistance. An unsatisfactory return having been received, a regiment was immediately raised and marched to the disputed territory.

Towards defraying the expense of this expedition New York advanced £5,000. The French were not unsuccessful and war was considered again commenced.

Three operations were decided upon: the first, an attack on Fort du Quesne, the second on Fort Niagara, and the third on Crown Point. The governor requested means to build another fort on the Hudson, and additional fortifications on the frontiers. But under the provisions of the late act of parliament any new issue of paper money was forbidden. Taxation was already oppressive, and a strong feeling existed against any further burden of this nature. These circumstances, said the general assembly, "render it impracticable for us to raise such further sums as appear necessary, in any other manner than by paper emission. But to emit bills of credit without making them a lawful tender we are confident will be absolutely useless, and without effect, for we are fully persuaded that no man in the province will be willing to accept that for money which he knows that another may refuse to receive as money from him, and if a law even under this restriction must have its execution suspended till his majesty's pleasure can be known, this his majesty's loyal colony may fall a prey to some ambitious, avaricious enemy before any return can be made." In answer to which objections the governor recommended the legislature to pass a law with the suspending clause, "the bills to be declared not a legal tender for debts contracted in Great Britain." The house refused to adopt his suggestion, and an adjournment was made. In the meantime advices were received from England, a proclamation for reassembling was issued, and soon after hearing and considering the governor's speech a bill was introduced and subsequently passed,[1] raising by tax £45,000, issuing for immediate use bills of credit for the like amount. They were put on the same footing as other bills of the province, and their currency continued until Nov., 1761.

The disastrous campaign of 1755-56 now opened. As a preliminary, Forts Beausijour and Gaspareau in Nova Scotia, were taken by some eastern troops, thus subduing the French in that province, but a succession of defeats followed, which more firmly established the French domination in America. The expedition against Fort du Quesne was a failure. Fort Edward was lost, as were Forts Granby and William Henry. Forts George and Oswego

[1] Feb. 19, 755.

were taken and demolished. The only defeat of the opposing forces was that at Lake George. The plan for connecting the northern and southern possessions by a line of forts succeeded, and the French now held undisturbed possession of all the country west of the Alleghany monuntains.

In prosecuting this campaign heavy drafts were made on the resources of New York. Paper money enactments followed each other in rapid succession. Besides the amount authorized on the 19th of February, ten thousand pounds were issued May 3d, eight thousand pounds Sept. 11th, ten thousand pounds April 1,1756, and fifty-two thousand pounds additional at the same date. This addition of £125, 000 to the debt of the province in two years, affected materially the character of the currency, and created some alarm in the general assembly. Unable to cancel the bills as they became due, they were repeatedly extended. A committee of the the house was instructed to bring in bills "for establishing a stamp office on vellum parchment and paper which should be charged with duty," and another "for laying an excise on all teas of foreign growth which should be sold by retail in the colony." Both measures were adopted.

The losses and disappointments of the last campaign greatly discomforted the crown and parliament of Great Britain, and their pride and courage arose in proportion. Mr. Pitt had just been placed at the head of a new ministry, and his active spirit invigorated all with whom he became engaged. In a circular to the colonial governors he informed them of his majesty's determination to send a large force to America to operate against the French, and called upon them to raise as large a force as possible.

However much the provinces may have been disheartened and borne down by previous misfortunes, their sympathies seemed at once engaged. To the call the general assembly of New York responded as follows: "With the utmost satisfaction we receive his majesty's directions for making an irruption into Canada, and we cannot entertain the least doubt that every colony on the continent will most heartily cöoperate with, and second his majesty's intentions by a vigorous exertion of their utmost strength." They agreed without hesitation to make effectual provision for levying, clothing, and paying such a body of troops as the number of inhabitants would allow. The plan was to raise 20,000 provincials, the king furnishing arms, ammunition, tents, and provisions. The number apportioned to New York was 2680 men, for the clothing and paying of whom £100,000 were emitted[1] in paper money, to be canceled by a nine years' tax.

The struggle then began, and its results are matters of well known history. Success attended it

[1] March 24, 1758.

through. It commenced by taking from the French, Louisbourg, then Fort Frontenac and soon after Fort du Quesne. Fort Stanwix was built, and Ticonderoga taken. The French were again defeated at Niagara, the fort taken, and finally Quebec fell.

Further appropriations were called for as the war advanced. A second issue of £100,000 of bills was made in 1759,[1] to be cancelled with the last, and in the same year[2] the sum of £150,000 was, at the request of Gen. Amherst, advanced to the British contractor's agent in America for supplying the army, for the immediate payment of which, paper money was emitted, on the credit of sets of bills of exchange drawn at 60 days, for 375,000 Spanish milled dollars. In 1760[3] the sum of £60,000 in further payment of the expenses of the 2680 men was added to the amount already issued, making a total of £410,000.

The amount of paper money in circulation had become large. In some of the colonies, and indeed in New York, the provisions for canceling as the bills matured, were not always adequate. It was ascertained upon an examination by a committee of the general assembly, that above £600 which should have been redeemed, were still in circulation. In some of the neighboring provinces such neglect was so serious as to constitute one of the chief causes of

[1] March 7th.

[2] July 3d.

[3] March 22.

depreciation, and was likewise the occasion of frequent and urgent complaint by British creditors. The agent of New York informed the general assembly that upon the complaints of divers merchants trading in Virginia, the lords commissioners of trade and plantations seemed determined to adopt the plan of the act passed during the reign of the late king, for regulating and restraining the paper currencies of New England, and to propose that the same should be extended over all the other colonies of North America. Despite our remonstrances against such a proceeding, parliament passed "an act to prevent paper bills of credit hereafter to be issued in any of his majesty's colonies or plantations in America from being declared to be a legal tender in payment of money, and to prevent the legal tender of such bills as are now existing from being prolonged beyond the periods limited for calling in and sinking the same."

The New York assembly, through their agents in England and Governor Moore, applied to the crown to have these restrictions removed, because the bills then in circulation would be sunk in 1768, and the country left without any medium for commerce, there being but little silver, on account of the interruptions of the Spanish trade. Governor Moore wrote also to the lords of plantations requesting instructions as to how far he might be authorized to give relief to the people in this case, so as to put them upon a footing with the neighboring colonies where the circulation of the paper credit was extended to more distant periods. The latter recommended that the governor be released from the restriction of not assenting to any law for issuing paper bills of credit whatever; that if found necessary a further sum of £250,000 might be issued under proper regulations and restrictions, but they refused to remove the restrictions of the legal tender, as that could not be done without the interposition of parliament.

The only currency that had up to this date been made a legal tender in the province of New York, consisted of Lyon dollars, and the paper bills of credit.[1] The former at this date (1768) were rarely seen, and the currency of the bills already issued would expire, as above stated, in the fall of 1768, after which time therefore there would be no legal tender. To relieve this serious difficulty, the general assembly passed an act making gold and silver coin a legal tender, fixing no value other than that for which they passed current in the common course of business; but as this would conflict with an act passed in the 6th of Anne, in regard to the value of different species of money, the governor refused his assent. Debtors became exposed to the malice of their creditors, and a clamor soon arose which induced the assembly, notwithstanding the recent

[1] The bills of the neighboring colonies were never made a legal tender in New York.

act of parliament, to pass a law emitting paper money to the amount of £120,000. It was similar to the preceding, except in one or two particulars. First, it was not to take effect until after the 1st of Nov., 1769, which would afford an opportunity to submit it for royal approval. Secondly, the interest of five per cent was to be paid on the whole capital for the first four years, and in the fifth year one tenth part of the capital to be sunk, and continued in the same proportion every succeeding year. To this act, on the petition of the assembly and council, the governor gave his assent; first, because the money could not be disposed of without the concurrence of the governor and council, and secondly because it had the effect of establishing a revenue for a number of years, an approach to a luxury which had not been recently enjoyed, and it was thought best not to despise it. The royal approbation was, on the same grounds, strongly urged in its behalf. There was some delay in responding to the communication of Governor Moore, and in the meantime Lt. Governor Colden succeeded to his office. He urged an approval of the measure which the assembly seemed to "have much at heart," stating that unless it was granted it would be difficult to make tbem continue the provision for the soldiers quartered in the province, after Massachusetts and South Carolina had both absolutely refused to do it. Having waited more than a year for the assent of the king, a new bill was introduced and passed, similar in its provisions with the last *without* the suspending clause, but providing that the bills should not be issued before the first of June following. There was a disposition to avoid all legislation of a public nature until the governor should give his assent to this bill, which he accordingly did, and for which he was afterwards severely reproved. The committee of the privy council, to whom both bills had been referred, reported unfavorably, and they were finally rejected on account of their inconsistency with the late act of parliament relating to legal tenders. An intimation was at the same time held out that parliament would probably pass a law enabling the legislature of New York to carry into execution the law for which they seemed so desirous. Such an act was passed the same year.[1]

In the fall of 1770 the £120,000 bill was again introduced, amended, and passed on the 16th of February following.[2] The money was loaned among the several counties for 14 years, at five per cent.

[1]An act to enable the governor and council and assembly of his majesty's colony of New York to pass an act of assembly for creating and issuing upon loan, paper bills of credit to ascertain amount, and to make the same a legal tender in payment into the loan offices and treasurer of the said colony.

[2]These bills were extensively counterfeited, so that a law was passed in 1773 substituting new bills. The matter of devising suitable devices &c., was referred to a committee. In the assembly

The general assembly continued its sittings until April 3d, 1775, when the country was in a state of revolution. The provincial congress of New York which succeeded the general assembly, arose out of a recommendation of the continental congress for each colony to organize a government for itself. It assembled on the 20th of April, 1775, and continued its session until January, 1778. It administered the government of New York during that period, and its resolutions and orders constituted our laws. In conducting the great struggle of the revolution, it experienced in common with other provinces and the continental congress the exceeding difficulty of procuring money for the subsistence of a suffering army.[1] Early in its session a committee was appointed to take into consideration the expediency of emitting a paper currency, which committee immediately prepared and presented (May 30, 1775) an elaborate report.

The conclusions formed were, that there was a smaller amount of gold and silver in this colony than in several others, and that it would be imposssi-

the following was proposed: "an eye in a cloud,—a cart and coffins,—three felons on a gallows,—a weeping father and mother with several children,—a burning pit, human figures forced into it by fiends, and a label with these words—Let the name of the money maker rot." The penalty of the law—capital punishment—was in several cases carried out. *See* papers of that date.

[1] During the Revolution our revenue officers were in the hands of the British.

ble to collect a sufficient sum without issuing a paper currency of some sort. Three modes were proposed by which it could be issued. First: that every colony should strike for itself the sum apportioned or to be apportioned by the continental congress.

Second: that the continental congress should strike the whole sum necessary and each colony become bound to sink its proportionate part.

Third : that the continental congress should strike the whole sum and apportionate the several shares to the different colonies, every colony becoming bound to discharge its own particular part, and all the colonies to discharge the part which any particular colony should be unable to pay.

The first proposition was disapproved of because the money issued would not have a general credit; the second was objectionable because default might be made by some of the colonies in sinking the amount assigned to it. The third was conceded to have the advantage of a higher and more general credit than either of the former, and the convention on the recommendation of their committee adopted it, and instructed our delegates in congress accordingly. The plan was not adopted by the continental congress, and the provincial congress resorted to an issue of £45,000 on the 2d of Sept., 1775. Other issues followed increasing the amount to £300,000.[1]

[1]May 5, 1776, £55,000; Aug. 30th, 1776, £200,000. In 1799 an act was passed canceling all bills issued by this congress of the denomination of one dollar and under.

Concerning the precise objects for which these sums were appropriated it is not necessary to make an account. The country was flooded with the emissions made by the several colonies and by the continental congress, and the evils produced were incalculably great. The country was unable to redeem its currency and the depreciation was ruinous. The whole amount issued in New York from 1709 to the last issue in 1786 was not large, and the special and repeated methods of taxation adopted for its extinction were as successfully carried out as the resources of the country would allow.

In 1781 an act was passed establishing the rate of depreciation of continental bills of credit, in the settlement of accounts.[1]

After the adoption of our state constitution in 1777, only two laws were passed making bills of credit; one in 1781,[2] for $411,250 to pay the proportion called for by congress towards the expenses of the war, and the other in 1786,[3] for £200,000 to be loaned at 5 per cent, for the purpose of increasing the currency.

[1] See table at the end of this work.

[2] March 27.

[3] April 18th.

The bills of the provincial congress as well as the continental bills were made a legal tender,[1] but in 1781 an act was passed, repealing all laws making bills of credit a legal tender, and four years later, all such bills in the state treasury were destroyed.

[1] Made so in 1780 at the rate of 8*s.* to the dollar. The money of account of the U. S., that is to say, the dollar, dime, cent, mill, was adopted in New York by an act passed Jan. 27, 1797, by providing that a dollar should be 4-10 of a pound, a dime 1-10th, &c., &c.

A
CATALOGUE
OF THE
BILLS OF CREDIT ISSUED BY NEW YORK
FROM
1709 TO 1789:
WITH A DESCRIPTION OF THE BILLS, THE DATES, DENOMINATIONS AND SIGNERS.

BILLS OF CREDIT.

1709.—June 8.

Amount, £5,000.

Form: This indented Bill of.........Shillings due from the Colony of New York to the Possessor thereof, shall be, in Value equal to Money; and shall be accordingly accepted by the Treasurer of this Colony, for the time being, in all publick payments; and for any Fund at any Time, in the Treasury. Dated, New York, Thirty-first of May, One Thousand Seven Hundred and Nine; by Order of Lieutenant-Governor, Council, and General Assembly, of the said Colony.

Signed by Lawrence Reade, Robert Walters, John Depeyster, and Robert Lurting, or any three of them.

Description: Indented at the top,—dated,—the arms of the city of New York on the left side, towards the bottom.

Number and division of the bills:

400	bills, each of	£5.
600	do.	40 shillings.
600	do.	20 do.
1,000	do.	10 do.
2,800	do.	5 do.

Currency limited to May 31, 1711.

Commissioners for canceling, the signers and treasurer.

Number canceled not known.

1709.—November 1.

Amount, £4,000 or 14,545 Lyon dollars.

Form: This indented Bill of.........Shillings, due from the Colony of New York to the Possessor thereof, shall be in Value equal to Money, and shall be Accepted accordingly by the Treasurer of this Colony for the time being, in all Publick Payments, and for any fund at any time in the Treasury. Dated, New York the First of November, 1709, by order of the Lieutenant Governor, Council, and General Assembly of the said Colony.

Signed by Robert Walters, John De Peyster, Robert Lurting, and Johannes Jansen, or any three of them.

Description: The same as of June 8.

Number and division of the biils:

400 bills, each of £5.		
400	do.	50*s*.
800	do.	25*s*.

Currency limited to Nov. 30, 1712.

Commissioners for canceling, the signers and treasurer.

1709.—November 12.

Amount, £4,000 or 14,545 Lyon dollars.

Form: This indented Bill of........Ounces of Plate, or.........Lyon dollars, due from the Colony of New York to the Possessor thereof, shall be, in value, equal to Money; and shall be accepted accordingly, by the Treasurer of this Colony for the Time being, in all publick Payments; and for any Fund, at any Time, in the Treasury. Dated in New York, the first Day of November, One Thousand Seven Hundred and Nine, by order of the Lieutenant Governor, Council and General Assembly of the said Colony.

Signed by Robert Walters, Robert Lurting, Johannes Depeyster, and Johannes Jansen, or any three of them.

Description: The same as of June 8.

Number and division of the bills:

300	bills, each of	20	Lyon dollars.
300	do.	16	do.
300	do.	8	do.
337	do.	4	do.

Currency limited to Feb. 28, 1713.

Commissioners for canceling, the signers and treasurer.

1711.—July 26.

Amount, £10,000.

Form: This indented Bill of.........Coyned Plate, due from the Colony of New York, to the Possessor thereof, shall be in Value equal to money, and shall be accepted accordingly, by the Treasurer of this

Colony, for the time being, in all publick payments, and for any fund in the Treasury. Dated in New York the 20th Day of July, 1711, by order of the Governor, Council and General Assembly of the said Colony.

Signed by Robert Walters, Robert Lurting, John Depeyster.

Description: Dated, and indented at the top, the arms of the city of New York on the right hand side towards the bottom.

Number and division of the bills:

500	bills, each of	20	ounces of plate.
500	do.	10	do.
1,000	do.	5	do.
500	do.	2½	do.
1,000	do.	2	do.
1,000	do.	1	do.
1,000	do.	½	do.
1,000	do.	¼	do.

Currency continued to 1724.

Commissioner for canceling, the treasurer.

1714.—September 4.

Amount, £27,680.

Form: This indented Bill of......... Ounces of Plate or.........due from the Colony of New York, to the Possessor thereof, shall be in Value equal to Money, and shall be accepted accordingly, by the

Treasurer of this Colony for the Time being, in all publick Payments, and for any Fund at any time in the Treasury. Dated in New York, the first day of July One Thousand Seven Hundred and Fourteen, by Order of the Governor, Council and General Assembly.

Signed by Robert Walters, Robert Lurting, David Provoost, and John Cruger, or any three of them.

Description: Impressed on the left side, about the middle of the side, the arms of the city of New York; the quantity of plate and the value of the same printed at the top.

Number and division of the bills:

568	bills,	each of	£10.
500	do.	do.	7 10*s*.
700	do.	do.	6.
720	do.	do.	5.
1,000	do.	do.	3.
800	do.	do.	2 10*s*.
800	do.	do.	1 10*s*.
1,000	do.	do.	1 5*s*.
1,200	do.	do.	15*s*.
1,500	do.	do.	15*s*.
2,000	do.	do.	6*s*.
4,000	do.	do.	3*s*.

Currency continued to Dec. 31, 1739.

Commissioners for canceling, the signers.

Amount canceled, £27,406 8*s*. 0*d*.

1715.—July 5.

Amount, £6,000 or 15,000 oz. of plate.

Form: Same as last, excepting the date.

Signed by Robert Walters, John Cruger, David Provoost, John Read, or any three of them.

Description: Same as last.

Number and division of the bills:

200 bills,	each of	£10.
200	do.	5.
200	do.	4.
200	do.	2.
1,000	do.	20*s*.
1,000	do.	10*s*.
1,200	do.	5*s*.

Currency continued to July 1, 1724.

Commissioners for canceling, the signers.

1717.—December 23.

Amount, £16,607 or 41,517½ oz. of plate.

Form: This Bill of......... ounces......... Penny-Weight of Plate, due from the Colony of New York to the Possessor thereof, shall be in Value equal to Sevil, Pillar, or Mexico Plate, and shall be Accepted accordingly by the Treasurer of this Colony for the time being, for all Publick Payments, and for any Fund at any time in the Treasury. Dated in New York, the twenty-eighth Day of November, One Thousand Seven Hundred and

Seventeen, by Order of the Governor and Council and General Assembly.

Signed by Robert Walters, Johannes Jansen, David Provoost, John Cruger, or any three of them.

Description: Impressed in the middle with the arms of the city of New York, and at the top of each, the quantity of plate represented.

Number and division of the bills.

1,391 bills,	each of	10 oz. of plate.	
1,000	do.	7 " 10 pwt.	do.
1,000	do.	5 "	do.
1,000	do.	2 " 10 "	do.
1,000	do.	2 "	do.
1,000	do.	1 " 10 "	do.
1,000	do.	1 " 5 "	do.
2,200	do.	1 "	do.
3,000	do.	15 "	do.
4,000	do.	10 "	do.
5,630	do.	5 "	do.

Currency limited to 1740.

Commissioners for canceling, the signers.

Amount canceled, £16,351.

1720.— November 19.

Amount, 5000 ounces of plate or £2,000.

Form: This indented Bill of.........Pennyweight ....Grains of Plate, due from the Colony of New York to the Possessor thereof, shall be in value equal to Plate, and shall be accordingly accepted by the Treasurer of this Colony, for the time being, in the Treasury, Dated in New York, the tenth day of November, One Thousand Seven Hundred and twenty; by order of the Governor, Council and General Assembly.

Signed by David Provoost, John Jansen, Jusboac Kip, Gerardus Beekman or any three of them.

Description: Impressed on the right side, about the middle of the side with the arms of the city of New York.

Number and division of the bills:

6,001	bills, each of	2 pwt.	12 grs.	of plate.		
4,000	do.	3	"	18	"	do.
4,000	do.	6	"	6	"	do.
4,000	do.	7	"	12	"	do.
1,714	do.	8	"	18	"	do.

Currency continued to Sept. 1, 1733.

Commissioner for canceling, the treasurer.

Amount canceled, £1,896 8*s.* 6*d.*

1723.— July 6.

Amount, £2,140 or 5,350 ounces of plate.

Form: This indented Bill of......... Ounces, and ....Pennyweight of Plate, due from the Colony of New York to the Possessor thereof, shall be in Value equal to Plate, and shall be accordingly accepted by the Treasurer of this Colony for the Time being, in all publick Payments, and for any Fund at any time in the Treasury. Dated in New York, the second Day of July, One Thousand Seven Hundred and Twenty-three; by order of the Governor, Council and General Assembly.

Signed by David Provoost, Johannes Jansen, Jacobus Kip, John Cruger, Gerardus Beekman, or any three of them.

Description: Impressed on the middle, with the arms of the city of New York, and on the top of each, the quanity of plate represented.

Number and division of the bills:

243 bills,	each of 11 oz.	5 pwt.	of plate.
299	do. 8 "	15 "	do.

Currency limited to July 1, 1726.

Commissioners for canceling, the treasurer and signers.

Amount canceled, £2,122 10*s.* 0*d.*

1724.—July 22.

Amount, £3,000.

Form: This indented Bill, due from the Colony of New York, to the Possessor, shall pass current in all Payments, for ...., conformable to Law made by the Governor, Council and Assembly of the said Colony, Dated the Twenty-second Day of July, One Thousand Seven Hundred and Twenty-four.

Signed by David Provoost, Johannes Jansen, Jacobus Kip, John Cruger, Gerardus Beekman, or any three of them.

Description: Impressed on the right side with the arms of the city of New York; at the top, bottom and each side, the value of each bill, an oval blank at the top with the date of bill substituted.[1]

Number and division of the bills:

800 bills,	each of	12	shillings.	
800	do.	8	"	
1,000	do.	6	"	
2,000	do.	4	"	
2,000	do.	3	"	6 pence.
2,000	do.	3	"	
1,800	do.	2	"	6 "
2,000	do.	2	"	
3,000	do.	1	"	6 "
4,000	do.	1	"	

Commissioners for canceling, the same as last.

Amount canceled,— see next issue.

1724.—July 24.

Amount, £6,630.

Form: This indented Bill, due from the Colony of New York, to the Possessor, shall pass in all Payments for........., pursuant to an Act of the Governor, Council and Assembly of the said Colony. Dated the Tenth Day of July, 1724.

Signed by David Provoost, Johannes Jansen, Jacobus Kip, John Cruger, Gerardus Beekman, or any three of them.

[1] This emission was to replace torn and defaced bills.

Description: Indented; the value of each bill printed at the top, bottom and each side, and impressed on the left side with the arms of the city of New York.

Number and division of the bills:

250	bills, each of	£3 12*s*.
380	do.	3 4*s*.
800	do.	1 12*s*.
1,495	do.	14*s*.
3,000	do.	7*s*.
4,000	do.	3*s*. 9*d*.
5,000	do.	1*s*. 3*d*.

Currency limited to July 1, 1729.

Commissioners for canceling, the same as last.

Amount canceled: of the amount issued July 22, £3,000, and July 24, £6,630, amounting to £9,630, the sum of £9,469 16*s*. 6*d*. was canceled.

1726.—November 11.

Amount, £3,000.

Form: This Bill shall pass current in all Payments for ...., pursuant to a Law of the Colony of New York, November sixteenth, One Thousand Seven Hundred and Twenty-six.

Signed by Stephen De Lancey, Frederick Philipse, Anthony Rutgers, Robert Livingston, jr., or any three of them.

Description: Same as those issued July 22, 1724.

Number and division of the bills:

800 bills, each of		12 shillings.			
800	do.	8	"		
1,000	do.	6	"		
2,000	do.	4	"		
2,000	do.	3	"	6 pence.	
2,000	do.	3	"		
1,800	do.	2	"	6	"
2,000	do.	2	"		
3,000	do.	1	"	6	"
1,600	do.	1	"	3	"
2,000	do.	1	"		

Currency issued to replace defaced bills.

Commissioners for canceling, the county justices of the peace.

Amount canceled, £2858 18*s.* 6*d.*

Printed by William Bradford.

1730.—October 17.

Amount, £3,000.

Form : By a Law of the Colony of New York, this Bill shall pass, within the same, for ...., in all Payments, and in the Treasury. Dated October xx, 1730.

Signed by John Cruger, Philip Van Courtlandt, Frederick Philipse, Henry Beekman, or any three of them.

Description: same as those issued July 22, 1724.

Number and division of the bills:

4,000	bills, each of	2	shilling 6 pence.
2,000	do	5	"
2,000	do	10	"
1,000	do	20	"

Currency, issued to replace defaced bills.
Commissioners for canceling, the signers.
Amount canceled, £2,999 10*s*.
Printed by William Bradford.

1734.—November 28.

Amount, £12,000.

Form: This Bill, by Law, shall pass current in the Colony of New York, for........, in all Payments, and in the Treasury, New York, Fifteenth, November, One Thousand Seven Hundred and Thirty four.

Signed by John Cruger, Frederick Philipse, Cornelius Van Horne, Stephen Bayard, or any three of them.

Description: Impressed on the left side with the arms of the city of New York.

Number and division of the bills:

300	bills, each of	£10.
600	do.	5.
800	do.	3.
800	do.	2 or 40*s*.
1,000	do.	1 or 20*s*.
1,000	do.	10*s*.
2,000	do.	5*s*.

Currency limited to March 25, 1746.
Commissioner for canceling, the treasurer.
Amount canceled, £11,576 15*s*.
Printed by William Bradford.

1737.—December 16.

Amount, £48,350.

Form: By a Law of the Colony of New York, this Bill shall pass current for........December 10th, 1737.

Signed by James Alexander, Simon Johnson, Peter Schuyler, Peter Jay, or any three of them, and by the treasurer or loan officer.

Description: Impressed on the right hand side with the arms of the city of New York.

Number and division of the bills:

1,000	bills, each of	£10.	
2,000	do.	5.	
3,000	do.	3.	
4,000	do.	2.	
5,000	do.		20 shillings.
7,700	do.		10 "
10,000	do.		5 "

Currency extended to 3d Tuesday in April, 1768.

Canceled in the presence of the justices and supervisors of the counties where loaned.

Amount canceled, £43,153 15*s*.

Printed by John Peter Zenger; engraved by Chs. Le Roux.

1739.— October 25.

Amount, £10,000.

Form: Same as last, except date.

Signed by John Moore, William Roome, David Clarkson, Peter Jay, or any two of them and the treasurer.

Description: Impressed on the right side with the arms of the city of New York. The amount of the respective bills at the lower part thereof.

Number and division of the bills:

200 bills,	each of	£10.
400	do.	5.
500	do.	3.
500	do.	2.
1,000	do.	1 or 20*s.*
3,000	do.	10*s.*
4,000	do.	5*s.*

Currency limited to Nov. 1, 1767.

Amount canceled, £9,115 6*s.*

Printed by William Bradford.

1746.— May 3.

Amount, £13,000.

Form: By a Law of the Colony of New York, this Bill shall pass current for........New York, the Tenth of May, One Thousand Seven Hundred and Forty Six.

Signed by Cornelius Van Horne, Paul Richard, Henry Cruger, Robert Livingston, or any three of them.

Description: Impressed on the left side with the arms of the city of New York.

Number and division of the bills:

650	bills, each of	£10.
650	do.	5.
650	do.	3.
650	do.	2.

Currency limited to the first Tuesday of January, 1748.

Commissioners for canceling, the signers and treasurer.

Amount canceled, £12,618 12*s*.

Printed by James Parker.

1746.—July 15.

Amount, £40,000.

Form: Same as the last, except the date July 21.

Signed by Cornelius Van Horne, Paul Richard, Abraham Lynsen, Isaac DePeyster, or any three of them.

Description: Impressed on the right hand side, with the arms of the city of New York, and under the Arms "Its Death to counterfeit this Bill."

Number and division of the bills:

1,861	bills, each of	£10.	
1,860	do.	5.	
1,860	do.	3.	
1,860	do.	2.	
1,860	do.	1.	
1,860	do.		10 shillings.

Currency limited to the first Tuesday of January, 1756.

Commissioners for canceling, the signers and treasurer.

Amount canceled, £38,772 10*s*.

Printed by James Parker.

1747.— November 25.

Amount, £28,000.

Form: Same as the last, except date.

Signed by Cornelius Van Horne, Paul Richard, Abraham Lynsen, Isaac DePeyster, or any three of them.

Description: Impressed on the left hand side with the arms of the city of New York, and underneath "Its death to counterfeit this Bill."

Number and division of the bills:

1,200	bills, each of	£10.	
1,250	do.	5.	
1,250	do.	3.	
1,250	do.	2.	
3,500	do.		20 shillings.

Currency limited to Nov. 25, 1756.

Commissioners for canceling, David Jones, Cornelius Van Horne, Paul Richard, and Henry Cruger.

Amount canceled, £27,098.

Printed by James Parker.

1755.—February 19.

Amount, £45,000.

Form: Same as the last, except date.

Signed by Isaac DePeyster, Oliver DeLancey, Nicholas Gouverneur, John Livingston, or any three of them.

Description: Same as those of July 15, 1746.[1]

Number and division of the bills:

2,094	bills, each of	£10.	
2,092	do.	5.	
2,092	do.	3.	
2,093	do.	2.	
2,092	do.	1.	
2,092	do.		10 shillings.

Currency limited to the first Tuesday of Nov., 1761.

Commissioners for canceling: In the year 1753, the speaker of the house of assembly and four members from New York, were appointed standing commissioners for canceling all bills of the province, as they became due.

Amount canceled, £36,325.

Printed by James Parker.

1755.—May 3.

Amount, £10,000.

Form: Same as the last, except date.

[1] Owen Sullivan was executed in 1756 for counterfeiting paper money, probably of this date.

Signed by Gabriel Ludlow, Abraham Lynsen, David Clarkson, James DePeyster, or any three of them.

Description: Same as those of Nov. 25, 1747.

Number and division of the bills:

200	bills, each of	£10.	
200	do.	5.	
250	do.	4.	
300	do.	3.	
1,250	do.	2.	
1,100	do.		20 shillings.
2,000	do.		10 "
2,000	do.		5 "

Currency limited to the first Tuesday of November, 1762.

Amount canceled, £7,550 6*s.*

Printed by James Parker.

1755.—September 11.

Amount, £8,000.

Form: Same as the last, except date.

Signed by Frederick Philipse, Philip Livingston, Beverley Roberson, Leonard Lispenard or any three of them.

Description: Same as those of July 15, 1746.

Number and division of the bills:

200	bills, each of	£10.
300	do.	5.

Number and division of the bills (continued):

300 bills,	each of	£4.
300	do.	3.
300	do.	2.
1,000	do.	20 shillings
1,000	do.	10 "
1,200	do.	5 "

Currency limited to the first Tuesday of November, 1761.

Amount canceled, £6,489 2*s*.

Printed by James Parker.

1756.—April 1.

Amount, £10,000.

Form: Same as the last, except date.

Signed by Paul Richard, Henry Cruger, William Walton, John Watts, or any three of them.

Description: Same as the last.

Number and division of the bills:

1,000 bills, each of £10.

Currency limited to the first Tuesday of November, 1761.

Amount canceled, £7,640.

Printed by James Parker.

1756.—April 1.

Amount, £52,000.

Form: Same as the last, except date.

Signed by Robert R. Livingston, John Cruger,

John VanDerSpiegel, William P. Smith, or any three of them.

Description: Same as the last.

Number and division of the bills:

2,200	bills, each of	£10.
4,000	do.	5.
2,000	do.	3.
1,000	do.	2.
2,000	do.	1.

Currency limited to the first Tuesday of November, 1766.

Amount canceled, £41,990.

Printed by James Parker.

1758.—March 24.

Amount, £100,000.

Form: Same as the last, except date.

Signed by Peter Van Brugh Livingston, David Clarkson, David Van Horne, Henry Cuyler, Jr., or any three of them.

Description: Same as the last.

Number and division of the bills:

8,000	bills, each of	£10.
4,000	do.	5.

Currency limited to the first Tuesday of November, 1768.

Amount canceled, £66,155.

Printed by James Parker.

10

1759.—March 7.

Amount, £100,000.

Form: Same as the last, except date.

Signed by Nathaniel Marston, John Morin Scott, Lawrence Reade, Andrew Barclay, or any three of them.

Description: Same as the last.

Number and division of the bills:

5,000	bills, each of	£10.
6,000	do.	5.
10,000	do.	2.

Currency, same as the last.

Amount canceled, £71,876.

Printed by William Weyman.

1760.—March 22.

Amount, £60,000.

Form: Same as the last, except date.

Signed by John Bogert, Jr., Robert G. Livingston, Elias DesBrosses, John Van Horne, or any three of them.

Description: Same as the last.

Number and division of the bills:

2,500	bills, each of	£10.
3,000	do.	5.
10,000	do.	2.

Currency, same as the last.

Amount canceled, £41, 970.

Printed by William Weyman.

1770.—Jan. 5.

Amount, £120,000.

Act repealed by the king, February 14, 1770.

1771.—February 16.

Amount, £120,000.

Form: By a Law of the Colony of New York, this Bill shall be received in all Payments in the Treasury for........., New York, the.........day of ....one thousand, seven hundred and seventy-nine.

Signed by Henry Holland, Walter Franklin, Theophylact Bache, Samuel Verplanck, or any three of them.

Description: Impressed with the arms of the city of New York, on the right hand side.[1]

Number and division of the bills:

5,000	bills, each of	£10.	
6,000	do.	5.	
6,000	do.	3.	
5,000	do.	2.	
6,000	do.	1.	
8,000	do.		10*s*.
8,000	do.		5*s*.

Amount canceled, not known.

Printed by Hugh Gaine.

[1]These bills were largely counterfeited. An act was passed in 1773, directing the signers to cause new plates to be prepared and 44,000 impressions struck off on thin paper and pasted over on the reverse side of the bills first emitted.

1775.—September 2.

Amount, £45,000 or $112,500.

Form: This bill shall pass current in all payments in this Colony for.........Spanish milled dollars, or the value thereof in gold or silver, according to the resolution of the Provincial Congress of New York, the second day of September, 1775.

Signed by Robert Ray, John Sebring, Evert Bancker, John Reade, John Broome, Jeremiah Brewer, Eleazer Miller, Thomas Tucker, William Denning, Abraham Brinckerhoff, Garrit Abeel, Abraham Livingston, Anthony L. Bleecker, William Mercey, or any three[1] of them.

Description: Impressed with the arms of the city and such other devices as the committee shall direct.[2]

Number and division of the bills:

5,000	$10 bills.
5,000	5 do.
5,000	3 do.
5,000	2 do.
10,000	1 do.
5,000	50 cent do.

Currency limited ½ to March 1, 1776; ½ to March 1, 1777.

[1] Afterwards reduced to two.

[2] Counterfeited in Westchester county.

The amount canceled of this and the two succeeding issues, was £133,477 17*s.* 8*d.*

Printed by J. Holt.

1776.— August 13.

Amount, 200,000 or $500,000.

Form: This bill shall pass current in all payments in this State for.........Spanish milled dollars, or the value thereof in gold or silver, according to the resolution of the Convention of New York, on the 13th day of August, 1776. *Excepting* those of the denomination of $\frac{1}{4}$, $\frac{1}{8}$, or $\frac{1}{16}$ of a dollar, which were in the form following:

This bill shall pass current in all payments in this State for Two shillings (or one shilling or six pence), being equal to ($\frac{1}{4}$ or $\frac{1}{16}$) of a Spanish milled dollar or the value thereof in gold or silver, according to the resolution of the Convention of New York, on the 13th day of August, 1776.

Signers not named.

Description: Same as last, with the addition "tis death to counterfeit."

Number and division of the bills:

20,000	$10 bills.
20,000	5 do.
20,000	3 do.
20,000	2 do.

Number and division of the bills (continued):

105,866	$\frac{1}{2}$ dollar bill.	
105,867	$\frac{1}{4}$	do.
105,867	$\frac{1}{3}$	do.
105,868	$\frac{1}{16}$	do.
6,000	$\frac{1}{9}$	do. for an extra.

Emission of the last session.

Printed by S. Loudon.

1776.—March 5.

Amount, £55,000 or $137,500.

Form: Same as the last, except the date.

Excepting: Those of the denomination of $\frac{2}{3}$, $\frac{1}{3}$, $\frac{1}{4}$, $\frac{1}{6}$, $\frac{1}{8}$ of a dollar, which were in the form following:

This bill shall pass current in all payments in this Colony for five shillings and four pence (or two shillings and eight pence, or two shillings, or one shilling and four pence, or one shilling), being equal to one-third (or $\frac{1}{4}$ or $\frac{1}{6}$ or $\frac{1}{8}$) of a Spanish milled dollar, or the value thereof in gold or silver, according to the resolution of the Provincial Congress of New York, on the 5th day of March 1776.

Signers not named.

Device, as the committee should direct.

Number and division of the bills:

2,350	$10 bills.
2,350	5 do.
2,350	3 do.
2,350	2 do.

Number and division of the bills (continued):

30,000	1	dollar bills.
30,000	$\frac{2}{3}$	do.
30,000	$\frac{1}{2}$	do.
30,000	$\frac{1}{3}$	do.
30,000	$\frac{1}{4}$	do.
30,000	$\frac{1}{6}$	do.
24,000	$\frac{1}{8}$	do.

Currency limited $\frac{1}{3}$ to March 1, 1779; $\frac{1}{3}$ to March 1, 1780; $\frac{1}{3}$ to March 1, 1781.

Printed by S. Loudon.

1781.—March 27.

Amount, $411,250.

Form: The Possessor of this Bill shall be paid ....Spanish milled Dollars by the thirty-first day of December, One Thousand Seven Hundred and Eighty Six, with interest from the 15th day of June 1780, in like Money, at the rate of five per cent per Annum, by the State of New York; and the first Payment of Interest to be on the 15th day of June, 1782, according to an Act of the Legislature of the said State, of the......Day of......1781.

Signed by

Amount canceled, $397,000.

1786.—April 18.

Amount, £200,000.

Form: By a Law of the State of New York, this

Bill shall be received in all Payments into the Treasury for.........New York, the......day of......... One Thousand Seven Hundred and Eighty six.

Signed by Evert Bancker, Henry Remsen, Jonathan Lawrence, John DePeyster, William Heyer, or any two of them.

Description: Impressed with the arms of New York on the right hand side.

Number and division of the bills:

6,000	$10	bills.
4,000	5	do.
6,000	4	do.
10,000	3	do.
10,000	2	do.
24,000	1	do.
20,000	10	shilling bills.
48,000	5	do. do.

Currency limited to June, 1800.

Amount canceled, $185,165 10*s*.

1788.

As the bills of the issue of 1786 were largely counterfeited, the legislature in 1788 (Feb. 8) passed an act creating new bills to be substituted for such of them as were still in circulation. They were similar to the last excepting the date, and the addition of the words, "tis death to counterfeit."

Signed by Daniel McCormick, Hendrick Wyckoff, John DePeyster, Nicholas Hoffman.

RECAPITULATION.

DATE.	AMOUNT ISSUED. £.	s.	d.	AMOUNT CANCELED. £.	s.	d.
1709...	5,000	0	0	Not Known.		
1709...	4,000	0	0	do.		
1709...	4,000	0	0	do.		
1711...	10,000	0	0	do.		
1714...	27,680	0	0	27,406	8	0
1715...	1,200	0	0	1,190	5	0
1717...	16,607	0	0	16,351	0	0
1720...	2,000	0	0	1,896	8	6
1723...	2,140	0	0	2,122	10	0
1724...	3,000	0	0	9,469	16	6
1724...	6,630	0	0			
1726...	3,000	0	0	2,858	18	6
1730...	3,000	0	0	2,999	10	9
1734...	12,000	0	0	11,576	15	0
1737...	48,350	0	0	43,153	15	0
1739...	10,000	0	0	9,115	5	0
1746...	13,000	0	0	12,618	10	0
1746...	40,000	0	0	38,772	10	0
1747...	28,000	0	0	27,098	0	0
1755...	45,000	0	0	36,325	0	0
1755...	10,000	0	0	7,550	6	0
1755...	8,000	0	0	6,489	2	0
1756...	10,000	0	0	7,640	0	0
1756...	52,000	0	0	41,990	0	0
1758...	100,000	0	0	66,155	0	0
1759...	100,000	0	0	71,876	0	0
1760...	60,000	0	0	41,970	0	0
1771...	120,000	0	0			
1775...	45,000	0	0	133,477	17	8
1776...	55,000	0	0			
1776...	200,000	0	0			
1781...	$411,250*			$397,001†		
1786...	£200,000	0	0	£185,165	10	0
Total,....	£1,655,857	0	0			

* Or £164,500.
† Or £158,800.

11

A

LIST OF ACTS

PASSED BY THE LEGISLATURE OF NEW YORK

RELATING TO

PAPER CURRENCY

FROM

1709 TO 1789.

LIST OF ACTS.

1709.—June 8: An act for the currency of bills of credit for five thousand pounds.

Nov. 1: An act for the currency of bills of credit for four thousand pounds.

Nov. 12: An act for the currency of bills of credit for ten thousand ounces of plate, or fourteen thousand five hundred and forty-five Lyon dollars.

1710.—Nov. 25: An act to retrench the growing interest of bills of credit.

1711.—July 26: An act for the currency of twenty-five thousand ounces of plate.

1714.—Sept. 4: An act for paying and discharging the several debts and sums of money claimed as debts of this colony, to the several persons therein named, and to make and enforce the currency of bills of credit, to the value of twenty-seven thousand six hundred and eighty pounds, for that purpose; also to make void all claims and demands made, or pretended to be due from this colony, before the first day of June, one thousand seven hundred and fourteen, and to prevent this colony from being in debt for the future.

1715.—May 19: An act explaining the act of 1714.

July 5: An act for a supply to be granted to his majesty for supporting his government in the province of New York, and for striking bills of credit for that purpose.

1717.—Dec. 23: An act for paying and discharging several debts due from this colony, to the persons therein named: and for raising and putting into the hands of the treasurer of this colony, several quantities of plate, to be applied to the public and necessary uses of this colony, and to make bills of credit to the value of forty-one thousand five hundred and seventeen ounces and a half of plate, for that purpose.

1720.—Nov. 19: An act for continuing the currency of bills of credit to the value of six thousand ounces of plate for and during the time therein mentioned.

Nov. 19: An act for a supply to be granted to his majesty for supporting his government in the province of New York, during the time therein mentioned, and for repealing an act of the general assembly of this province, for a supply to be granted to his majesty for supporting his government in the province of New York, from the first day of July which shall be in the year of our Lord, one thousand seven hundred and twenty, until the first day of July, one thousand seven hundred and twenty-one.

1721.—July 27: An act for the further continuing the currency of bills of credit to the value of six thousand ounces of plate, for and during the time therein mentioned.

1722.—June 22: An act for making more effectual, an act entitled, an act for a supply to be granted to his majesty for supporting the government in the province of New York etc. (passed Nov. 19, 1721.)

July 7: An act for continuing the currency of bills of credit to the value of three thousand ounces of plate, till the first day of July which will be in the year of our Lord, one thousand seven hundred and twenty, to the first day of July, which will be in the year of our Lord, one thousand seven hundred and twenty-four.

Nov. 1: An act for raising the quantity of three thousand ounces of plate, for the effectual sinking and canceling bills of credit to that value.

1723.—July 6: An act of raising and levying the quantity of five thousand three hundred and fifty ounces of plate, for the uses therein mentioned, and for striking and making bills of credit of that value.

1724.—July 24: An act for raising and levying the sum of six thousand six hundred and thirty pounds, for supplying the deficiencies of his majesty's revenue, and for the several uses and purposes therein mentioned, and for making of bills of credit to be issued for that value.

July 24: An act for making bills of credit, and putting the same into the treasurer's hands, for changing therewith such bills of credit of this province as are torn and defaced.

1725.—Nov. 10: An act for continuing bills of credit struck and issued in the year one thousand seven hundred and twenty, to the value of five thousand ounces of plate, to be current until the first day of July, which will be in the year one thousand seven hundred and twenty-seven.

1726.—June 17: An act for the further continuing the currency of bills of credit, struck and issued in the year one thousand seven hundred and twenty, to the value of five thousand ounces of plate, until the first day of July, one thousand seven hundred and twenty-eight.

1727.—Nov. 11: An act for striking bills of credit to the value of three thousand pounds, and putting them into the treasury, to be exchanged for shattered, torn and defaced bills struck and issued by virtue of the several acts therein mentioned.

1728.—Aug. 31: An act to continue the currency of bills of credit struck and issued in the year one thousand seven hundred and twenty, to the value of five thousand ounces of plate until the first day of July, one thousand seven hundred and twenty-nine.

1729.—July 12: An act to continue the act last mentioned for one year.

1730.—Oct. 17: An act for striking bills of credit to the value of three thousand pounds, and putting them into the treasury, to be exchanged for shattered, torn and defaced bills struck and issued by virtue of several former acts.

Oct. 17: An act for the further continuing the currency of the bills of credit struck and issued in the year one thousand seven hundred and twenty, to the value of five thousand ounces of plate during the time therein mentioned.

1732.—Oct. 14: An act to repeal the act, and to cancel the bills of credit therein mentioned, and to grant unto his majesty several duties for supporting his government in the colony of New York, until the first day of September, which will be in the year of our Lord, one thousand seven hundred and thirty-seven.

1734.—Nov. 28: An act to strike and make current bills of credit to the value of twelve thousand pounds, on the funds, and for the uses therein mentioned.

1735.—Nov. 8: An act to revive, enforce and continue the currency of bills of credit therein mentioned until the end of the year one thousand seven hundred and thirty-nine.

1737.—Dec. 16: An act for emitting bills of credit for the payment of the debts, and for the better support of the government of this colony, and for other purposes therein mentioned.

1739.—Oct. 25: An act further to continue the duty of excise, and the currency of the bills of credit emitted thereon; and to strike some new bills for exchanging such old ones as are or may be unfit to circulate.

1740.—Nov. 3: An act to cancel the bills of credit emitted in the year 1715, 1720, 1723, 1724.

1743.—Dec. 17: An act to prolong the currency of bills of credit emitted by virtue of an act entitled, an act for emitting bills of credit for the payment of the debts and for the better support of the government of this colony, and for other purposes therein mentioned.

Sept. 1: An act explaining the last mentioned act.

1746.—May 3: An act for raising a supply of the sum of thirteen thousand pounds, by a tax on estates real and personal, for the more effectual fortifying this colony; for the emitting bills of credit for the like sum for the immediate answering the necessary services, and for sinking and canceling the said bills at the several short periods therein mentioned.

July 15: An act for raising a supply of forty thousand pounds, by a tax on estates real and personal, for carying on an expedition against the French in Canada; for emitting bills of credit for the like sum, and for sinking and canceling the said bills in short periods, and for other purposes therein mentioned.

1747.—Nov. 25: An act for raising a supply of twenty-eight thousand pounds, by a tax on estates real and personal for defraying the expense of several services necessary for the defence of the frontiers and annoyance of the enemy: for emitting bills of credit for the like sum, and for sinking and canceling the said bills in short periods.

1748.—April 8: An act for the more effectual canceling the bills of credit of this colony.

1750.—Nov. 24: An act further to prolong the currency of bills of credit emitted by virtue of an act entitled, an act for emitting bills of credit for the payment of the debts, and for the better support of the government of this colony, and for other purposes therein mentioned.

1753.—July 4: An act to amend an act entitled, an act for the more effectual canceling the bills of credit of this colony.

July 4: An act further to continue the duty of excise, and the currency of bills of credit emitted thereon, for the purposes in the former act, and herein mentioned.

1755.—Feb. 19: An act for raising a supply of forty-five thousand pounds by a tax on estates real and personal, for putting this colony into a proper posture of defence, for furthering his majesty's designs against his enemies in North America, and other, the purposes therein mentioned; for emitting bills of credit for the like sum, and for sinking and canceling the said bills in short periods.

May 3: An act for paying and subsisting eight complete companies of one hundred effective men each, officers included, to assist in conjunction with the neighboring colonies in erecting one or more forts nigh Crown Point, within his majesty's dominions: for raising the sum of ten thousand pounds, for and towards the said services, and for making current bills of credit to the amount thereof, and other the purposes therein mentioned.

Sept. 11: An act for raising the sum of eight thousand pounds, to be contributed to the colony of Connecticut, towards the expense of a reinforcement of two thousand effective men, now levying in the said colony, for the army destined against Crown Point under Major General Johnson; and for emitting bills of credit to the amount of the said sum of eight thousand pounds, for making immediate payment.

1756.—April 1: An act for the payment of the debts due from this colony, and for other purposes therein mentioned.

April 1: An act for raising, paying and subsisting one thousand seven hundred and fifteen effective men, officers included, to be employed in conjunction with the neighboring colonies on an expedition for reducing the French fort at Crown Point, and carrying on an offensive war against the Indians who infest the western frontiers of this colony, and other purposes therein mentioned.

July 9: An act more effectually to suppress and prevent the counterfeiting of the paper currency of this colony.

Dec. 1: An act (continuing the act of Dec. 16, 1737).

1757.—Dec. 24: An act (continuing the act of Dec. 16, 1737).

1758.—March 24: An act for raising, paying, and clothing, two thousand six hundred and eighty effective men, officers included, for forming an army of twenty thousand men, with the forces of the neighboring colonies, to invade the French possessions in Canada, in conjunction with a body of his majesty's regular troops and other purposes therein mentioned.

Dec. 16: An act (continuing the act of Dec. 16, 1737).

1759.—March 7: An act for raising a supply of one hundred thousand pounds, for levying, paying, and clothing, two thousand six hundred and eighty effective men, officers included, for forming, with the forces of the neighboring colonies, an army of twenty thousand men, to invade, in conjunction with a body of his majesty's regular troops, the French possessions in Canada; for emitting bills of credit for the like sum, and for sinking and canceling the said bills in short periods.

July 3: An act for emitting bills of credit to the amount of one hundred and fifty thousand pounds, to enable his majesty's general to pay the debts contracted, and to carry on his majesty's service in North America, and for sinking the same within twelve months.

Dec. 24: An act (continuing the act of Dec. 16, 1737).

1760.—March 22: An act for levying, paying, and clothing two thousand six hundred and eighty effective men, officers included, for forming an army of twenty thousand men, with the forces of the neighboring colonies, to reduce in conjunction with his majesty's regular troops, Montreal, and other posts belonging to the French in Canada, for emitting bills of credit for the sum of sixty thousand pounds, and for sinking the said bills in short periods.

Nov. 8: An act (continuing the act of Dec. 16, 1737).

1761.—Dec. 31: An act (continuing the act of Dec. 16, 1737).

1762.—Dec. 11: An act (continuing the act of Dec. 16, 1737).

1763.—Dec. 13: An act (continuing the act of Dec. 16, 1737).

1770.—Jan. 5: An act for emitting the sum of one hundred and twenty thousand pounds, in bills of credit to be put out on loan, and to appropriate the interest arising thereon, to the payment of the debts of this colony, and to such public exigencies as the circumstances of this colony may from time to time render necessary. (Repealed by the king, Feb. 14, 1770).

1771.—Feb. 16: An act (title, same as last).

1773.—March 8: An act to remedy the evil this colony is exposed to from the great quantities of counterfeit money introduced into it.

1774.—March 9: An act to prevent the depreciating the paper currency of this colony.

1775.—April 3: An act to amend (the act of Feb. 16, 1771) so far only as it relates to the county of Suffolk.

1779.—Feb. 26: An act to cancel certain bills of credit of this state (of the denomination of $1 and under issued by the provincial congress).

1780.—March 1: An act to cancel the defaced bills of credit at this state.

June 20: A supplementary act to the act entitled, an act approving of the act of congress of the 18th day of March 1780, relative to the finances of the United States, and making provision for redeeming the proportion of this state of the bills of credit, to be emitted in pursuance of the said act of congress.

Oct. 7: An act to procure a sum in specie, for the purpose of redeeming one sixth part of the bills emitted on the credit of this state, pursuant to the act of congress of the 18th day of March, 1780, for discharging the interest of such bills, and for other purposes therein mentioned.

1781.— Feb. 22: An act for the better establishing the rate of exchange between the bills emitted upon the credit of this state, pursuant to the act of congress of the 18th of March, 1780, and the continental currency theretofore issued.

March 27: An act for emitting moneys upon the credit of this state.

July 1: An act to repeal such of the laws of the state which make several emissions of bills of credit a legal tender.

1785.— March 14: An act for canceling the bills of credit therein mentioned.

1786.— April 18: An act for emitting the sum of two hundred thousand pounds in bills of credit for the purposes therein mentioned.

May 1: An act supplementary (to the above).

1788.— Feb. 8: An act to take out of circulation the bills of credit emitted by law, and to emit others as a substitute.

1789.— Feb. 20: An act directing the treasurer of this state to cancel certain bills of credit and certificates therein mentioned, and for the further direction of the loan officers.

Rate of Depreciation of Continental Bills of Credit, as fixed by an Act of the Legislature of New York, passed March 30, 1781, for the payment of Debts and the Settlement of Accounts.

DATE.	Sum requir-ed to pay $100.	Per cent of value.	DATE.	Sum requir-ed to pay $100.	Per cent of value.
1777, Sept. 1,	100	100	1778, Dec. 15,	679	14
" 15,	104	96	1779, Jan. 1,	742	13
Oct. 1,	109	91	" 15,	796	12
" 15,	115	87	Feb. 1,	868	11
Nov. 1,	121	83	" 15,	932	10.7
" 15,	127	79	Mar. 1,	1000	10.0
Dec. 1,	133	75	" 15,	1048	9.5
" 15,	139	72	Apr. 1,	1104	9.0
1778, Jan. 1,	146	68	" 15,	1156	8.7
" 15,	152	65	May 1,	1219	8.2
Feb. 1,	160	63	" 15,	1272	7.8
" 15,	167	59	June 1,	1344	7.4
Mar. 1,	175	57	" 15,	1404	7.1
" 15,	186	53	July 1,	1436	6.9
Apr. 1,	203	49	" 15,	1548	6.5
" 15,	214	46	Aug. 1,	1631	6.1
May 1,	230	43	" 15,	1709	5.8
" 15,	245	40	Sept. 1,	1800	5.5
June 1,	265	37	" 15,	1908	5.2
" 15,	281	35	Oct. 1,	2032	4.9
July 1,	303	33	" 15,	2151	4.6
" 15,	332	30	Nov. 1,	2340	4.3
Aug. 1,	348	28	" 15,	2433	4.1
" 15,	370	27	Dec. 1,	2597	3.8
Sept. 1,	400	25	" 15,	2741	3.6
" 15,	429	23	1780, Jan. 1,	2932	3.4
Oct. 1,	464	21	" 15,	3115	3.2
" 15,	500	19	Feb. 1,	3333	3.0
Nov. 1,	545	18	" 15,	3533	2.8
" 15,	584	16	Mar. 1,	3732	2.6
Dec. 1,	634	15	" 15,	4000	2.5

INDEX.

www.ingramcontent.com/pod-product-compliance
Lightning Source LLC
LaVergne TN
LVHW021430110826
845150LV00007B/2163

* 9 7 8 1 4 2 5 5 0 7 4 7 3 *